Amazed & Amused™

Survive & Thrive as a Healthcare Professional

Karyn Buxman, RN, MSN

Cover design & painting by Sally Poole
www.PooleAdvertising.com; 573-221-3635

Published by LaMoine Press

www.KarynBuxman.com
Karyn@KarynBuxman.com
800-848-6679

"Those who dance are thought mad by those who do not hear the music."
~ Ann Nonymous

Dedication

To my friends and colleagues
in the healthcare profession.
You rock.

amazed | uh 'mazd |
adjective

inspired to see the world through appreciative eyes; having
an expanded mindset, giving one a broader perspective on
life; astonished; affected with great wonder; filled with the
emotional impact of something wonderful and/or surprising.

amused | uh 'myoozd |
adjective

experiencing mild humor and gentle joy; having a mindset open to appreciating life's absurdities and quirkiness; experiencing a childlike delight; the ability to appreciate the humor in any situation.

Table of Contents

Introduction

I sat down recently with pen in hand to try to summarize the lessons I've learned as a nurse, and the perspectives I've gained as a keynote speaker. The result was the poem "Amazed and Amused." It definitely contains some insights, and it just might contain some wisdom.

A friend recently asked me how long it took to write. I told her it took one hour to write, and 50 years to live it and figure it out.

My mom was a nurse, my dad was a doctor, my sister is a doctor, and my brother is a respiratory therapist. It doesn't take a rocket scientist to see that healthcare was etched into my DNA. I became a nurse because, like so many of you, I wanted to help people.

When I first became a nurse almost 30 years ago, the work was hard but I loved what I did, I loved the people I took care of, and I loved the people I worked with. We did our jobs and we also managed to laugh everyday on the job. Each day brought something new, and I loved learning. And over time, the job got harder and the resources became tighter. People laughed less and less.

While teaching at a college of nursing and pursuing a graduate degree I found my calling in the field of humor. My masters thesis explored the relationship between humor, health and communication. I then immersed myself in the world of therapeutic humor. I also found that I was funny. Who knew?? My (unintentionally) funny academic presentations of my thesis evolved into a series of keynote speeches. And I evolved into a humorist keynote speaker.

Along the way I partnered with Doug Fletcher to bring to life the humor magazine for nurses, *The Journal of Nursing Jocularity*. I became actively involved in the Association for Applied and Therapeutic Humor. I partnered with Steve Wilson to co-found World Laughter Tour. I gave presentations in the U.S. and abroad for the

International Society of Humor Studies. I published my findings in journals such as *American Journal of Nursing, AACN Critical Care Issues, The Journal of Psychosocial Nursing* and *AORN*. I am also a contributing author of of *Chicken Soup for the Nurses Soul.* I have keynoted for the Mayo Clinic, MD Anderson, Scripps, ENA, ONS, AORN and hundreds of other companies and institutions.

Like most nurses, I spent many years juggling work and family. And while I pursued my mission on the forefront of my field, life continued on. My youngest son was stricken by a bizarre malady that lasted seven years; my oldest son was diagnosed with cancer; my mother developed Alzheimer's, and I went through a painful divorce.

At first I didn't see these experiences as valuable lessons. In fact, I didn't want these experiences *at all.* When you're in the midst of such times in your life, it's hard to have perspective. But my sons have recovered, my mother passed away and no longer suffers, and my new life has provided joys beyond my wildest imagination. Now I can grasp the lessons that came forth from those times. I understand how those same lessons can help and inspire others in all walks of life: *To think with an amazed and amused mind; to love with an amazed and amused heart, and to live with an amazed and amused spirit.*

The stories I hear from nurses continue to have two things in common: they are amazing and they are amusing. Occasionally someone will ask if one of my stories really happened. All nurses know that one does not have to make this stuff up—one does not even need to embellish! The stories, from the profound to the hysterical, stand on their own.

I still have my nursing license, although I now nurse nurses, rather than patients. And while I practice my profession in a way that is foreign to most, I still love nursing and will always be a nurse. And although my goal is to live life amazed and amused, I often end up dazed and confused. And I find that amazing and amusing.

~ *Karyn Buxman, RN*

Amazed & Amused

The Poem

To think with an Amazed and Amused mind —
To love with an Amazed and Amused heart —
To live with an Amazed and Amused spirit —
    This is to live, work and play well.
    (This is what everyone REALLY wants!)
    This is my wish for you.

To see the joy and wonder amid the pain—

In a baby's first cry

or a loved one's last breath.

*T*o be incredulous over your own uniqueness—

For never before, or ever again, will there be another

with your thoughts, your talents, your potential.

To marvel at the individuality of others

and the richness they bring to your life—

For they complement you

and they complete the work of the world.

*T*o be in awe of the exactness of a snowflake —
    To be speechless at the perfection of the universe
    and your place in the order of things.

To delight in a child's giggle—
A perfect cup of coffee,
your favorite song on the radio,
an unexpected windfall,
a penny on the sidewalk (head's-up, for good luck),
a falling star,
a good joke,
a smile from a stranger.

To be able to stand in your own pain—

Or in your own accomplishments, or in another's place

with a sense of wonder and amazement.

To be able to step back and observe your

daily frustrations—

Or your own blunders, or another's bungling . . .

with a sense of amusement.

T o celebrate your strengths and embrace

your weaknesses—

For the wise understand that both have a place,

'tho why is not obvious at first.

To accept that some things are hard-wired,

while others are optional —

> *And to accept the challenge of figuring-out*
>
> *which is which*
>
> *in the inconsistent conglomeration that is*
>
> *your personality.*

To laugh 'til you cry, and cry 'til you laugh —
Cleansing your body of tension
and washing your emotions clean.

To jump on your bed, sing in the rain,
dance in the street—

To risk feeling silly and foolish;
for stepping out of your comfort zone is a small
but sure step in achieving positive change.

*T*o be present for someone in need —

   To speak from your heart, to speak the Truth . . .

      or to not speak at all, but to simply be there.

To grasp the game of life —

To play hard, win gracefully and lose honorably . . .

and get up to play again and again and again.

To speed-up, slow-down, or go-backwards—
Whatever is required at the moment
to keep yourself moving forward.

$\mathcal{T}$o live for today, not waiting for those rare

peak experiences—

To celebrate your comfortable routines

and embrace the surprises of life.

To feel what you're feeling—

And to express it when appropriate, and harbor it

when necessary . . .

But to feel it nonetheless.

To live in the moment, appreciating the Now—

But to not lose sight of the past and the future,

which create the context of your life.

To be consistent-yet-contradictory—

   To strive to improve yourself

      and still accept yourself as you are.

$\mathcal{T}$o buy your ticket and take the ride —

To ride the rollercoaster with the wind in your hair,

to walk through the haunted house with your heart

in your throat.

*T*o play at your work and work at your play—

Realizing that work without meaning is death,

and play without purpose is . . . fun!

To know your own heart and your own mind —
   To know when to listen to the whisper of
      your emotions,
   and when to heed the call of logic.

To live in alignment with your own

personal philosophy—

To stand firm in your own beliefs

yet honor the differences in others.

To listen —truly listen —to what others have to

say—

    And also hear what they fail to say,

        yet need to communicate so very badly.

To talk and shout and whisper and sing and hum—
To speak in your own voice, whether quietly or loudly;
To sing your own song, no matter how strong or weak
or out of key.

To simplify and focus your life —

To clear away the clutter, the distractions, the barriers;

To embrace the core, the essence, of what really matters to you.

To find your "work-play"—

That which you would work at joyfully

regardless of the pay, the recognition or reward.

To grow in wisdom, not merely in years—
To experience knowledge turning into wisdom,
and memories turning into guidance.

To find friends and be a friend —

    To laugh until it hurts,

    to cry on each other's shoulder,

    to share confidences,

    to revel in each other's successes,

    to endure each other's failures,

    to be there come hell or high water.

To embrace, acquire and absorb knowledge—

From books, teachers and experience;

through eyes, ears and years.

*T*o lighten up —

> To grin 'til your cheeks hurt
>
> Chuckle 'til you can't talk
>
> Snort 'til milk comes out your nose
>
> Giggle 'til you're out of control
>
> Guffaw 'til folks ask you to keep it down
>
> Belly laugh 'til you double up and fall over
>
> Laugh 'til you cry and cry 'til you laugh.

To slow-down, shut-up and pay-attention —

For there is wisdom in the silences

as well as in the voices and books.

$\mathcal{T}$o stand in astonishment at your mind and body—

At your brain, the most complex two-pounds of

matter in the universe;

and at your body, a biomechanical and

engineering wonder.

To embrace seeming negatives, trusting that they will turn out for the best—

> To see the humor in life's absurdities.
> To be able to laugh at yourself.

To have an attitude of gratitude and a
   forgiving spirit.
To cast off resentment and regret.
To practice acts of kindnress—
   random or otherwise.

To live each day Amazed and Amused —

This is to achieve true success.

This is to attain lasting significance.

This is experience genuine happiness.

Amazed & Amused

Musings

Amazed

It's amazing what a little ingenuity can accomplish . . .

Sophie, a patient with Alzheimer's, had developed a bad habit of wandering into dangerous or restricted areas of the nursing home, such as the kitchen, the loading dock and the basement.

Nothing but constant survellience would stop her.

Then one day one of the nurses noticed that Sophie always avoided a round, black throw rug. Inspiration struck, and the nurse bought several of the rugs, and placed them in front of all the restricted areas.

It worked like a charm, as Sophie perceived the round, black rugs to be holes in the ground!

Amused

Harold, a cute five-year-old boy, was in the hospital for a kidney transplant. He understood his condition, and was looking forward to the life-saving operation.

But after a visit from his doctor, he began crying uncontrollably. His parents couldn't console him, and they couldn't get him to explain why he was upset.

Finally, the transplant coordinator sent Harold's parents from the room so she could talk with him alone. She comforted him and gave him the opportunity to ask questions. Finally, between snuffles, he asked quietly, "Is this kidney coming from a boy or a girl?"

"What difference would that make?" she asked.

"Because . . . because—*I don't want to have to sit down to pee!*"

Amazed

Not that you asked . . . But do you know what amazes me? It amazes me that hotels still don't have thirteenth floors.

First: Are *that* many people truly superstitious?

Second: Do they really think they're fooling anyone?? I mean, if you were superstitious, would you stay on the "fourteenth" floor?

Third: Hospitals *do* have thirteenth floors. Hmmm . . .

Amused

A nurse once told me this story:

As a staff nurse on a busy neurological unit, I would go on morning rounds with the resident. Each person's level of orientation was assessed with questions like, "What day is it?" "What month is it?" and "Where are you?"

Later in the day, I was making the bed in one of the patient's rooms. We had a casual conversation as the gentleman watched me work. As I put the pillowcase onto the pillow, he blurted out, "You can't do it *that* way!"

Startled, I asked him to tell me what I was doing wrong.

He said, "You have to put the pillow case on so I can read the hospital name printed on the end." To answer my puzzled look he whispered: "Everyday the doctors come in and ask me where I am . . . *and I read it off the pillow case.*"

Amazed

A nurse colleague of mine was instructing a nervous young single mother on how to care for her child's tracheotomy. The mom was scared and very unsure of herself. She had little self-esteem, no familiarity with medical procedures, and few financial resources.

The nurse smiled and confidently proclaimed: "I'll work with you until you're so comfortable caring for your son's trach that people will mistake you for a respiratory therapist!" The young mom smiled weakly.

The mom learned, the boy recovered successfully, and we heard nothing more from them. Until two years later . . . When we received an invitation to attend the mom's graduation from a local college, where she'd completed the program certifying her to be a respiratory therapist.

Amused

Several American nurses were training at a hospital in Liverpool, England. These nurses had little money for meals, so they ate the awful food provided at the hospital complex. Sometimes kindly visitors would give them some of the treats they had brought for patients.

One night a visitor brought a homemade pie to the hospital. She said to one of the American nurses, "Would you eat this up, love?" The nurses were excited and grateful, and they wasted no time in devouring the delicious pie.

The woman returned 15 minutes later and asked, "Is me 'usband's pie 'ot yet, dearie?"

Amazed

I'm amazed that a good light bulb joke will still bring down the house . . .

How many doctors does it take to change a light bulb?

Nobody knows . . . They just ask the nurses to do it.

How many nurses does it take to change a light bulb?

Just one . . . But at the same time she's charting notes, passing meds, hanging blood, changing sheets, emptying bedpans, answering calls, admitting patients, discharging patients, greeting families, helping docs, pacifying administrators, satisfying Joint Commission, juggling paperwork, explaining procedures, answering lights, running here, dashing there, being everywhere, deciphering orders, skipping meals, monitoring IVs and performing CPR!

Amused

After working as a nurse in ICU for a couple of years, I became pregnant and delivered a precious baby boy. I took a leave of absence and threw myself into my new domestic role.

I became an expert on every aspect of infant care and breastfeeding. One afternoon, after nursing my son, I took him with me Christmas shopping to a nearby jewelry store. While browsing, the owner, a long-time family friend came over and admired the baby. He then looked at me and asked, "Are you still nursing?"

I was somewhat surprised that this gentleman would be interested in the fine art of breast feeding, but assured him that although at times it was inconvenient, it was very good for the baby and very fulfilling for me.

There was an uncomfortable silence . . . and then I noticed his sales-clerk, who was a bright shade of red, turn and walk toward the back of the store. As I looked at the jeweler again, it finally dawned on me that he wasn't inquiring about the womanly art of breast-feeding . . . he merely wanted to know if I was going to return to work!

Amazed

When my older son, David, was a junior in college, he was diagnosed with cancer. The doctor told him that without chemotherapy and surgery, he would die. David's attitude was amazing and amusing, and no doubt played a role in his complete recovery.

Prior to his diagnosis, he'd worked part time as a bouncer in a bar. He and his fellow bouncer had been dubbed by their friends as "The Lone Ranger" and "Tonto."

Following one of his chemotherapy sessions, a bunch of his buddies came by to visit. After they cleared out, David smiled and announced, "My friends just gave me a new nickname: Chemo-Sabi!"

Amused

YOU KNOW YOU'RE A NURSE IF . . .

10. You find yourself staring at other customer's arm veins in grocery check-out lines.

9. Your sense of humor seems to get more warped each year.

8. Your bladder can expand to the size of a Winnebago water tank.

7. You can intubate your friends at parties.

6. You don't get excited about blood loss . . . unless it's your own.

5. You live by the motto, "To be right is only *half* the battle; to convince the physician is the *rest* of the battle."

4. You've basted your Thanksgiving turkey with a Toomey syringe.

3. You've told a confused patient your name was that of a co-worker . . . and to HOLLER if they need help.

2. Every time you see a patient's bed you have an overwhelming desire to lie down in it.

1. You believe every patient needs "TLC"—that's *not* "Tender Loving Care," but "Thorazine, Lorazepam and Compazine."

Amazed

My younger son, Adam, suffered through a bizarre illness during his entire adolescence. Several times a day he was hit with massive migraine-like headaches which threw him to the floor with epileptic-like seizures, then left him partially paralyzed for an hour.

We tried every therapy known to mankind, and visited medical centers around the country. Nothing helped, and nobody knew what to do. Adam became a medical mystery, and his case attracted research scientists, doctors and neurologists from around the world.

The malady was, at times, overwhelming, but Adam's spirit never ceased to amaze me. One day while in a hospital in Chicago, neurologists stood outside his door—like kids lined up at a candy store—just waiting to get their turn at my son, the medical mystery.

One neurologist entered the room and, without so much as an introduction or "Hello," proceeded to set up a pile of sophisticated recording equipment. He sat down and began firing questions, head bent over his pad—no eye contact, no smile, no beside manner whatsoever.

The questions were repetitious and left Adam bored. Then, the doctor posed a question that he'd never been asked before. "Have you ever experienced Déjà Vu?"

Without missing a beat, Adam leaned toward the doctor and quipped, "Didn't you just ask me that?"

Amused

A man goes to his doctor and says, "I think my wife's hearing is failing. What should I do?"

The doctor replies, "Try this test to find out for sure. When your wife is in the kitchen doing dishes, stand 15 feet behind her and ask her a question. If she doesn't respond, keep moving closer in five-foot intervals, and repeat the question until she hears you."

The man goes home and sees his wife preparing dinner. He stands 15 feet behind her and says, "What's for dinner, honey?"

He gets no response, so he moves five feet closer and asks again.

Still no response . . . so he moves another five feet closer. He asks again. And again, no answer.

Finally he stands directly behind her and says, "Honey, what's for dinner?"

She replies, "For the *fourth* time, I SAID CHICKEN!"

Amazed

Isn't it amazing that . . .

An average adult has 2,500,000,000,000 red blood cells.

100,000,000,000 new red blood cells are created every *day*.

An individual blood cell circumnavigates a body in 20 to 60 seconds.

An average human scalp has about 100,000 hairs on it.

A human being loses an average of 40 to 100 strands of hair a day.

A person will die from total lack of sleep sooner than from starvation. Death will occur after about 10 days without sleep, while starvation takes several weeks.

By the time you turn 70, your heart will have beat approximately 2,500,000,000 times.

Laughing lowers levels of stress hormones and strengthens the immune system.

Six-year-olds laugh an average of 300 times a day. Adults only laugh 12 to 55 times a day.

Amused

As part of the admission procedure in the hospital where I once worked, I asked patients if they were allergic to anything. If they were, I would print it on an allergy band placed on the patient's wrist.

Once when I asked an elderly woman if she had any allergies, she told me that bananas made her lips swell.

Imagine my surprise when, several hours later, the woman's irate son stormed up to the nurses' station and demanded to know, "Who is responsible for labeling my mother 'bananas'?"

Amazed

"I need to ask your advice about something important," my mom said. She hesitated. "I need to know how I can tell the difference between those two men at my house. The ones who look so much alike."

My heart sank. My mom and dad lived alone. Her confusion was the latest manifestation of the Alzheimer's that was slowly overtaking her.

"Which men?" I asked slowly.

"You know. There's LaMoine, your dad, and there's that *other* man who looks just like him. I can't tell the two of them apart, and I don't know which one to trust. What should I do??"

I panicked for a moment. Then an inspiration of gentle humor and common sense came to me, and I said: "Just call out 'LaMoine!' If he answers 'What, Shirley?' then it's Dad. But if he answers, 'Who's LaMoine?' then that's the *other* guy."

I held my breath. Then a smile spread slowly across my Mom's face. She said softly and seriously, "Yes . . . that should work. I can do that." Then she turned to me and, with tears in her eyes, said, "Thank you, honey."

Despite my deep sadness, I also felt a a warm gratitude for our momentary connection. Sometimes logic is illogical, and gentle humor is our amazing and amusing grace.

Amused

Doctors at a major hospital had gone on strike. Hospital officials said that they will find out what the doctors demands are—as soon as they can get a pharmacist over there to read the picket signs.

Amazed

After my divorce, I felt that my travel schedule would probably rule out finding another man in my life. But just in case, in my journal, I wrote a list of the qualifications of my soul mate—two pages, single spaced. (I wanted to make sure I'd recognize him if he *did* show up!) Among my qualifications was "Romance. Romance. Romance!"

Fast forward two years. An author/speaker colleague asked if he could take me to coffee to talk about the biz. As he had sold 3 million books, I figured I could pick his brain, too!

We sat down over coffee at 11:30 one Thursday morning and proceeded to chat. We talked of business and we talked about our lives. After a bit, he asked, "Do you need to get back home or would you like to grab some dinner?" I was puzzled. Why would he want to eat *again*? We'd just sat down. I looked at my watch—it was 7:00 pm! We'd been sitting in one spot for almost 8 hours, and the coffee shop was closing.

We walked a block and got pizza. "Ten minutes" later it was 11:30pm . . . a 12-hour coffee date! He asked me to coffee again the next day—and he showed up with a single long stem pink rose.

Nine months later he asked me to marry him at the very table where we'd had our first date. And you want to know what's *really* amazing? My husband, Greg Godek, is the author of the bestseller *1001 Ways to be Romantic!*

What would *you* call this?? Unbelievable? Astonishing? Amazing?!

Amused

TOP 10 CHARTING CHUCKLES

10. Patient fell in November and has been going downhill ever since.

9. The patient had waffles for breakfast and anorexia for lunch.

8. Exam of genitalia wsas completely negative except for the right foot.

7. The skin was pink to the touch.

6. She is numb from her toes down.

5. She broke her hip when whe slipped and fell on a wet floor. She is practically blind and didn't notice the floor.

4. Rectal exam revealed normal sized thyroid.

3. Both breasts equal and reactive to light and accommodation.

2. Patient refused autopsy.

1. Patient deserves colonoscopy.

Amazed

While traveling across the country on a 22-city tour with the World Laughter Tour in 1999, my colleague Dr. Madan Kataria and I visited a kindergarten class in Phoenix. I introduced myself, saying, "I'm Karyn Buxman, from Hannibal Missouri," and I pointed to a U.S. map. "And *this* is Dr. Madan Kataria who has traveled all the way from Mumbai, *India*! Does anyone know where India is?"

Immediately, the air was full of wildly-waving arms, and shouts of "Pick me! Pick me! I know! Pick me!" I pointed to a little boy in the front row and asked, "Okay, son, where's India?"

He lit up for a moment and then scrunched up his face and moaned dramatically through his fingers, "I . . . forgot!" A little girl, unable to contain herself shouted triumphantly, "It's right here in Phoenix!"

I responded slowly, "Hmmm . . . I don't *think* so—" Not missing a beat, the girl threw her hands up in the air and said emphatically, "Well, it *used* to be!"

Later I recalled the experience and marveled at how every child had jumped at the opportunity to participate. They didn't hesitate for a nano-second. They weren't thinking, "What if I don't have the right answer?" or "What if someone thinks I'm stupid?" They just wanted to have fun and participate.

It's amazing what we can learn from children, isn't it?

Amused

Isn't it funny how many famous "doctors" there are in the world??

Dr. Seuss

Dr. Frankenstein

Dr. Pepper

Dr. No

Dr. Dre

Dr. Zachary Smith

Dr. Doom

Dr. Kildare

Dr. Watson

Rex Morgan, M.D.

Dr. Huxtable

Dr. Who

Dr. Strangelove

Amazed

One day after presenting a seminar with my friend and colleague, Doug Fletcher, publisher of *The Journal of Nursing Jocularity*, I stopped by his hotel room on our way out. Before we left his room, Doug paused to shove a handful of loose change in between the cushions of the couch.

I watched this curious behavior in baffled amazement. "What on *earth* are you doing?" I asked.

He turned and grinned from ear to ear. "We're not gonna be here to *see* it, but some day someone is going to have *so much fun* finding the money in this couch!"

I shook my head, thinking to myself, "You need a hobby."

But on my flight home I marveled at Doug's creativity and attitude. It was simply brilliant. He didn't care that he wasn't going to be there to witness the event. He didn't care that he wasn't going to get credit for it. He did it simply because it was *fun*! And the very thought of it was funny!

So now . . . whenever I'm in a hotel room . . . I always shove a few coins in between the cushions of the couch. For fun and for Doug. And then—because I'm into immediate gratification!—I scatter a few coins on the floor.

Amused

A patient rang his call light. A nurse answered through the intercom: "May I help you?"

"Yes. Can you come to my room?"

"I'll be there in a minute."

After a brief pause the patient asked, "Is that a *real* minute or a *nurse's minute*?!"

Amazed

It was eight o'clock on a Monday morning. In my haste to get myself ready for the week, I'd temporarily forgotten about my seven-year-old son. A rhythmic thumping noise coming from upstairs finally brought him back to mind.

A mom-on-a-mission, I ran up the stairs. As I approached Adam's room I could feel the *"Whomp! Whomp! Whomp!"* vibrating through the walls. "What in the *world*—?!" I wondered.

I opened his door and saw Adam—wearing nothing but his underwear and a big smile . . . jumping up and down on his bed . . . singing and dancing . . . swinging his school clothes over and around his head . . . with enthusiastic kicks accenting the beat.

"What do you think you're doing, young man?" I demanded.

Adam stopped mid-jump, grinned a huge grin, and with the wisdom of Yoda, said, "Don't ya think getting dressed in the morning oughta be more fun, Mom?!"

These are the answers that flashed through my mind: "NO!!!" and "No more of Mommy's motivational tapes for *you*, young man!"

But the humor and wisdom of my son got through to me, and I realized that he was right. Wouldn't it be marvelous if we all could have more fun while getting dressed, getting up, going to work, doing the chores . . . ?! It's not about *what* you're doing—it's about your *attitude* toward it.

Amused

When a man from a nursing home came to the emergency department with pneumonia, the nurse contacted the next-of-kin listed on his chart. The patient's sister arrived the next day.

After explaining the patient's condition to his sister, the nurse asked her, "So, are you the closest relative?"

She replied, "Oh no, honey! I live clear in *Pennsylvania*!"

Amazed

You've heard it said that "There's no such thing as a stupid question." Well I'm not so sure about that . . .

A friend who works at the Miami Convention & Visitors Bureau once got this question from a tourist: "Which beach is closest to the water?"

A friend in Denver was once asked by a visitor: "What time of year do your deer turn into elk?"

Another friend in South Dakota overhead this beauty: "Is Mount Rushmore natural or manmade?"

My travel agent once booked a flight for a woman who had apparently never flown before. When asked if she wanted a window seat, the woman responded, "You'd better give me an aisle seat. I don't want to get my hair messed up."

And a colleague swears that this is true: At an office meeting, the manager asked if anyone would like to participate in the firm's 401K. An eager-but-naïve new employee said, "I think I might—but can you tell me how many miles that is?"

Amused

During a hospital fire drill, a nurse was closing doors to patients' rooms. An 86-year-old patient was talking on the phone when the nurse reached her room. As the nurse shut the door, the patient asked, "What's going on?"

"Don't worry," the nurse answered, "We're just having a little fire drill."

As the nurse was leaving, she heard the patient say into the phone, "No, dear, everything's just fine. The hospital is on fire but a nice little nurse just came to lock me in my room."

Amazed

The effects of laughter on the body . . . Amazing!

RESPIRATORY SYSTEM: Laughter increases respiratory activity and oxygen exchange.

CARDIOVASCULAR SYSTEM: Laughter stimulates heart rate and blood pressure followed by a relaxation phase; vasodilatation.

SYMPATHETIC NERVOUS SYSTEM: Laughter increases production of catecholamines, resulting in increased levels of alertness and memory, and enhanced learning and creativity.

IMMUNE SYSTEM: Immunoglobulin A found in significantly increased levels of saliva with stimulation of humor and laughter; increased spontaneous lymphocyte blastogenesis, a natural killer cell activity.

MUSCLE SYSTEM: Laughter stimulates muscles and reduces muscle tension, often resulting in diminished pain.

BRAIN: Laughter stimulates both hemispheres at the same time, coordinating all the senses and producing a unique level of consciousness and a high level of brain processing.

TEARS (of laughter or grief): Provides exocrine response, carrying away toxins found in cells under stress.

Amused

Ann, a home health nurse, met her new patient, Mr. Jones—a quiet man who had a gorgeous head of hair. His chemotherapy had the potential to cause hair loss, and Ann voiced her concern about how he might react if this were to happen. Mr. Jones just smiled and said he could handle it.

The next day, Ann returned for a follow-up visit. Mr. Jones' wife opened the door, looking quite upset. Mr. Jones sat in the living room, wearing a hat, and scowling.

"What's wrong?" asked Ann.

Mr. Jones growled, "You *said* I might lose some hair . . . but *this* is *ridiculous!*" He pulled off his hat to reveal that he was *totally bald.*

Ann gasped in horror.

She then noticed the smile breaking through Mr. Jones' frown. Ann looked over at his wife, who was smiling, too—and holding up his toupee!

Amazed

Some of the benefits of humor:

PSYCHOLOGICALLY, humor acts as a major coping mechanism; relieves anxiety and tension; serves as an outlet for hostility and anger; provides a healthy temporary escape from reality; and lightens heaviness related to illness, trauma and grief.

SOCIALLY, humor establishes rapport; decreases social distance; and lessens the hierarchy between individuals; is often referred to as a "social lubricant."

WITH COMMUNICATION, humor helps convey information; aids in negotiations; defuses difficult situations; creates bonds between people.

Amused

A nursing assistant, a floor nurse and a charge nurse were eating lunch together in the break room . . . when suddenly a Fairy Godmother floated into the room.

"I am so pleased with the work you're all doing that I will grant one wish to each of you!"

The nursing assistant jumped up first and said, "I wish I were on a tropical island beach with ten single, muscular men feeding me fruit and tending to my every need." The Fairy Godmother waved her magic wand, and the nursing assistant vanished in a puff of smoke.

Then the floor nurse, all excited, called out, "I wish I was rich and retired—and spending my days in my own cozy cabin at a Colorado ski resort with a handsome man feeding me cocoa and doughnuts." The Fairy Godmother waved her magic wand, and the floor nurse vanished in a puff of smoke.

The Fairy Godmother then turned to the third nurse and asked, "And what is *your* wish?"

Calmly and quietly, without even looking up from her sandwich, the charge nurse said, "I wish those two would be back on the floor at the end of the lunch break."

Amazed

The rank of death, among people's major fears: 2

The rank of speaking in public, among people's major fears: 1

The percentage of doctors who smoke: 15

The number of American who drink Coca-Cola for breakfast: 965,000

Percentage of people who say that nurses are honest and ethical: 84

Percentage of people who say that doctors are honest and ethical: 66

Amount that Americans spent on chocolate last year: $16,235,000,000

Percentage of all chocolate worldwide that's consumed by Americans: 23

Chance that an anti-depressant will alleviate severe depression: 1 in 2

Chance that a placebo will alleviate severe depression: 1 in 3

Amused

So . . . I just got TiVo. Now I can spend the rest of my life catching-up on old episodes of . . .

General Hospital

Doogie Howser, MD

Marcus Welby, MD

Dr. Quinn, Medicine Woman

St. Elsewhere

ER

Scrubs

Grey's Anatomy

Nightingales

Quincy

House

Doctor Kildare

Ben Casey

Chicago Hope

*M*A*S*H*

Amazed

I can recall in vivid detail the very first time I started an IV line solo. The patient was a burly young 25 year old man with veins the size of garden hoses. Awesome! The only drawback was his wife, who sat at the bedside, scrutinizing my every move. No problem, I thought. I was used to being observed by instructors.

I prepared my IV bag and tubing, laid out all my equipment, applied the tourniquet and prepared my site. I then smoothly inserted the angiocath into the bulging vein. Jackpot! I connected my tubing, secured it, taped the site, and adjusted the flow rate. Feeling successful and smug, I turned to the wife and said, "Everything is going fine."

She cocked her head, looked me straight in the eye and asked, "When are you going to take *that* off?" as she pointed at her husband's arm.

I panicked for a moment when I saw that the tourniquet was still wrapped tightly around the patient's now dusky blue-tinged arm. My brain went into overdrive. I smiled a reassuring smile to the wife as I held my watch up in front of me and studied it closely; my other hand on the end of the tourniquet. "Just a moment," I said and paused, pretending to count down. "Three, two, one—I can take it off . . . *now!*" and then snapped the tourniquet from his arm.

Having restored confidence in my patient and his wife, I left the room amazed that humor and quick wit were good for me *and* my patients.

Amused

As a young nurse I worked in a small hospital where it was easy to know the entire staff—from the docs and nurses to the dock workers and volunteers.

One morning while I was hurrying down the hallway to circulate for the next C-section, I saw a tall young man in scrubs looking somewhat lost. "Must be the soon-to-be father," I thought. Out loud I asked, "Are you looking for the C-section?"

He nodded. "Well, you can't go into the operating room without a mask! Follow me."

Silently he followed me to the sink, where I first showed him how to wash his hands, and then handed him a mask. "Here," I instructed him. "You take these two strings and tie them like *this* . . . and these two strings and tie them—like *so*!"

He nodded slowly, then replied, "I prefer to tie mine like *this*," and after demonstrating, he extended his hand. "I'm the new pediatrician, Dr. McHardy."

I smiled back, shook his hand enthusiastically, and said, "And I'm Nancy Roberts, the OR supervisor."

It was two weeks before he discovered that I'm *not* Nancy Roberts!

Moral of the story: Never let them see you sweat!

Amazed

As nurses thrive on chocolate, I thought you might want to know . . .

800,000,000 Hershey's Kisses are produced every day.

Hershey's Kisses were thus named because the machinery that places dollops of chocolate gently "kisses" the conveyor belt.

Christopher Columbus introduced chocolate to Spain in 1504. It took more than a century for the confection to make its way to Great Britain.

The Swiss consume the most chocolate (22.3 pounds per person per year); followed by the British (17.9 pounds per person per year); and Americans are in third place (12.6 pounds per person per year).

Cocoa beans contain a substance called theobromine, which is similar to caffeine; and phenylethyline, which is similar to amphetamine.

Some health experts say the purer the chocolate, the better it is for you. Chocolate with a cocoa content of more than 50% is high in magnesium, and contains calcium, potassium, sodium and iron. It also contains vitamins A_1, B_1, B_2, C, D and E.

The amount of glucose use by an adult human brain each day—measured in M&Ms—is 250.

Amused

Nursing administrators from several hospitals were lamenting the shortage of registered nurses. Desperate for a solution, one of the gals jokingly asked her colleagues to send her three RNs from each of their hospitals.

The following day this email appeared in all of their in-boxes:

"The nursing shortage calls for creative solutions. We have the answer to all of your staffing problems! Just send three of your RNs to each of the hospitals on the list below. Then add YOUR hospital to the bottom of the list. Then send this letter to five additional colleagues. Within 14 days you will receive 1,567 nurses. This really works! One hospital in India received specialists in every area they needed, and were able to replace all of their lazy nurses, including that one nursing supervisor whom everybody hated. Do not break this chain! If you do, bad luck will befall your unit. One administrator in Argentina broke the chain, and within a week her nursing staff went on strike, a fire broke out in the ICU, and her dog died."

Bio
Karyn Buxman, RN, MSN

Karyn Buxman is a registered nurse. She's *practiced* nursing in several hospitals in many units, and she's *taught* nursing, too. She now nurses nurses through her inspirational humorous speeches. Karyn is a best-selling author, a professional humorist, and an observer of the human condition. Her poem, "Amazed & Amused" captures her philosophy of life and work, and speaks to the hearts, minds and souls of nurses and other people worldwide.

Karyn holds a masters degree in nursing; her graduate work focused on the relationship between humor, health and communication. She recently was bestowed the Lifetime Achievement Award from The Association for Applied and Therapeutic Humor. Karyn is also one of only 33 women in the *world* to be inducted into the Speaker Hall of Fame. She has written for journals such as *AJN, AORN,* and *Journal of Psychosocial Nursing,* and has appeared in *Woman's Day,* and *Marie Claire.* She was a co-founder of *The Journal of Nursing Jocularity,* and is also a contributor to *Chicken Soup for the Nurses Soul.*

Karyn lives in La Jolla, California—where she takes sunset walks on the beach year-round, collecting sand dollars with her romantic husband—and spends each day amazed and amused . . . that life could be so much fun, endlessly surprising, and astonishingly beautiful.

Karyn presents keynotes that provide audiences
with insights cleverly disguised as humor.

For an amazing & amusing experience
please call!

800~848~6679
Karyn@KarynBuxman.com
www.KarynBuxman.com